FROM TO MENO TO POST MENOPAUSE:

A LOVE STORY

Eunice Gibson – Hudson

DEDICATION

This book is dedicated to my daughter, niece, and all women who will experience menopause symptoms, with the hope that it will shed light on their experience and make the transition easier. Menopause is a natural part of life that every woman will go through, and it is essential to understand the changes that occur during this time. Written as a love story, this book aims to empower women to take control of their health and well-being as they navigate the menopause journey with confidence and ease by providing information, practical tips, and emotional support.

ACKNOWLEDGEMENT

First and foremost, I would like to express my deepest gratitude to God for granting me the ability and inspiration to write this book. The divine guidance and strength provided by God have been instrumental in this creative endeavor.

I am also thankful for the profound insights on the menopausal transition that I gained during my certification study in Menopause with Girls Gone Strong (GGS). It provided me with valuable insights and information on menopause. The knowledge and understanding gained from their course have been instrumental in navigating this significant life transition.

My heartfelt appreciation goes to my husband for his unwavering support and understanding during my challenging period of menopausal symptoms. His patience and encouragement have been invaluable in enabling me to focus on this project.

I am also indebted to my daughter and niece for their constructive feedback on the manuscript. Their perspectives and input have contributed to refining the content and ensuring its relevance to a wider audience.

Finally, I would like to extend my gratitude to the countless women who have shared their stories and experiences with me. Their courage and openness along with my personal experience have allowed me to better understand the complexities of menopause and have given me the opportunity to create a book that is both informative and empathetic.

PREFACE

In the natural course of life, every woman undergoes menopause, a transformative journey encompassing perimenopause, menopause, and post-menopause. This book is a love story, a dedication to women who lack support and information during this phase, including my daughter and niece, aged 30 and 42. Through my personal menopausal journey, I share the challenges I faced at 43, encountering dismissive responses from doctors who attributed my symptoms to youth or suggested psychological causes.

Frustration heightened with emergency room visits, as symptoms like heart palpitations, vision disturbances, and fatigue raised concern. Only later did I realize these were manifestations of hormonal changes during menopause. I write to offer the support and information I wished for, empowering women to navigate this phase confidently.

This love story follows Hope, a woman in her mid-40s, on a self-discovery journey. Symbolically, Peri represents pre-menopause, Meno signifies menopause, and Post embodies post-menopause, as Hope's transformative journey unfolds.

The narrative underscores the importance of understanding menopausal symptoms, bridging the awareness gap, and embracing change with resilience. Through Hope's experiences, I aim to provide women with the knowledge I lacked, fostering confidence during this transformative phase. This book is not just a personal reflection but a beacon of support, encouraging women to approach menopause with understanding, resilience, and a sense of empowerment.

When life throws lemons, make something amazing with it to enjoy. Stressing is not the answer!

So, grab something comfortable to wear, to drink and sit back, relax, and ENJOY!

A Love Story: From Peri to Meno to Post, "Oo la la"

From Fun Dating to Settling Down

Once upon a time, there was a vibrant and adventurous woman named Hope who loved experiencing new things. She thoroughly enjoyed dating and meeting different men, as it allowed her to explore various aspects of life. Her interests ranged from traveling to dancing, sporting events to dining, partying to relaxing with people she found interesting. She embraced the idea of living her best life and cherished the moments she shared with these amazing men she met along the way.

As time passed, our heroine began to feel the pangs of growing older. While she had reveled in the excitement of her carefree dating life, she now longed for something more meaningful. At 45 years old, deep within her heart, she yearned to settle down and find the love of her life, someone with whom she could build a future and share her joys and sorrows.

In her quest for true love, our protagonist comes across a younger man in his early 40s named **Peri (Perimenopause)**, who seems to be the perfect match for her.

At first, Peri was amazing, and they shared a strong connection. They were destined to be together. Their initial encounter was nothing short of magical. Peri possessed an irresistible charm that drew her in effortlessly. They shared common interests, laughed at each other's jokes, and seemed to be in harmony.

Peri could be the one, she had been searching for all along.

Their bond grew stronger each day, and they became inseparable. They would take long walks together, exploring new places and trying new things. They would spend hours talking about their past experiences and sharing their aspirations for the future. Through it all, they found comfort and solace in each other's company.

The First Signs of Trouble

As time went on, Hope noticed that things were not as perfect as they initially seemed. She started to see cracks in their relationship and realized that Peri was changing and no longer the man she thought he was. There were unexpected disagreements, misunderstandings, and instances where Peri's behavior left her feeling hurt and confused.

Despite these issues, she tried to work through them, hoping that they could overcome the obstacles and find their way back to the happiness they once shared.

However, as their relationship progressed, problems intensified. Beneath Peri's charming exterior, he had certain flaws that started causing friction between them.

The Struggles and Challenges

Hope had experienced love and relationships in various forms, she now found herself going through a whirlwind of emotions and health issues in her relationship with Peri. These challenges took a toll on her physical and mental well-being, causing her to suffer from various symptoms such as irregular periods, insomnia, joint stiffness, fatigue, mood swings, and more. In her relationship with Peri, she also faced other struggles that caused her immense stress. This stress manifested in many ways, such as headaches, back pain, anxiety, sleepless nights and depression, which had never been an issue in her previous relationships.

The woman found herself torn between her desire to settle down and her realization that Peri might not be the right partner for her. She questioned whether it was worth sacrificing her dreams of finding true love just to avoid being alone. The journey towards self-discovery and understanding what truly mattered in life became her focus.

In the end, our protagonist makes a difficult decision. She chose to prioritize her own happiness and well-being over settling for a relationship that was not fulfilling her needs. She realized that finding the love of her life should never mean compromising on her own values and aspirations. After **five years** of dating, both Hope and Peri decided to break up as she transitioned into the next dimension of her love life. She was single again, but not for long.

Hope Meets Meno (Menopause)

After the breakup, Hope took some time to heal and rediscover herself. She focused on personal growth and self-reflection, learning valuable lessons from her past relationship with Peri. Little did she know that fate had something unexpected in store for her.

With newfound clarity, Hope continued her journey, remaining open to new possibilities and experiences. In her pursuit of self-love, she also understood that love could come in unexpected ways and at unexpected times. While she may have encountered obstacles along the way, she never lost hope that she would eventually find the person who would truly complement her life.

One day, while attending a social event, Hope crossed paths with a man named Meno (Menopause). He was just a little bit older than her at 50. There was an instant connection between them, and they quickly became close friends. At first, considering what she had gone through for the past 5 years, Meno was kind-hearted, understanding, and shared many similar interests with Peri.

As they spent more time together, their friendship gradually turned into something more profound (*no more monthly periods*).

Hope and Meno embarked on a new romantic journey filled with excitement and possibilities. They cherished each other's company and supported one another through thick and thin. However, as time passed by, they began to realize that their relationship was not as compatible as they initially thought.

They had different communication styles and struggled to find common ground on certain issues. They just stopped speaking to each other (in menopause, no more monthly periods).

Hope's experience with Meno was short-lived, as she realized that the relationship was not providing her with the happiness and understanding she needed. Like Peri, Meno had similar traits which caused tremendous stress in Hope's life. Such overabundance of stress resulted in her having night sweats, brain fog, joint pain, anxiety, heart palpitations, hot flashes, confusion, forgetfulness, inflammation and more. Despite their efforts to work through these challenges, it was a natural process for Hope and Meno to part ways after just **one year** of being together, leaving her feeling disheartened and questioning her ability to maintain a healthy relationship. Yet, it was a bittersweet transition for both, but they understood that sometimes what they consider love is just not enough to sustain a relationship.

They both called it quits and went their separate ways without words.

Hope Marries Post

After the breakup with Meno, Hope focused on herself once again. She continued to grow personally and emotionally, determined to find the love she truly deserved. Little did she know that her path would soon cross with an older man named Post.

Hope's journey led her to Post. There was an instant spark between them. They shared a deep connection and understood each other on a profound and mature level. Post was destined and God sent as he came with less baggage. Most of the time, he was very caring, and supportive, and had a similar vision for the future. Other times, he had his moments of communication issues, ignoring her and anger, but nothing that could not be worked out. Hope was still able

to focus on self-care, doing the things she loved, and enjoying life.

With both Post's challenges and support, she was able to overcome the challenges she faced in her previous relationships and live a happier, healthier life. She learned to accept that love is not void of complications, arguments or even setbacks. She developed better coping skills to ride the waves of being in a committed relationship.

As they got to know each other better, their love grew stronger (menopause symptoms got better), and they realized that they had found their soulmate.

Hope and Post decided to take their relationship to the next level and got married. They celebrated their love in a beautiful ceremony surrounded by friends and family. Their love story was a testament to the power of perseverance, growth, and finding true happiness.

The Moral of the Love Story

In conclusion, Hope's love story is a testament to the importance of finding understanding and supportive partners in life. By learning from her past experiences and focusing on self-care, Hope was able to overcome the struggles and challenges she faced in her relationships with Peri and Meno and find happiness with Post.

How does this apply to Menopause Transition?

The Menopause Transition: A Love Story of hope

The menopause transition is a significant phase in a woman's life, akin to a love story. In this narrative, Hope is the protagonist who dates three significant characters: Peri (perimenopause), Meno (menopause), and Post (post menopause). Each stage in Hope's journey is marked by distinct characteristics and experiences, much like the distinct stages in a love story.

Dating Peri: The Perimenopause Stage

During the perimenopause stage, Hope experiences the beginning of her menopause transition. Like the initial excitement and butterflies in a new relationship with Peri, perimenopause brings about irregular periods, hot flashes, and mood swings that will leave one feeling a mix of emotions, including frustration and anxiety, as her body undergoes changes.

In this stage,

Perimenopause: The Early Stage

Perimenopause usually begins in a woman's 40s, but it can start as early as the mid-30s for some individuals. This stage is characterized by fluctuating hormone levels, particularly estrogen and progesterone. Some common symptoms experienced during perimenopause include:

- ***Irregular periods***: Menstrual cycles may become shorter or longer, and the flow may be lighter or heavier than usual. Some women may also experience skipped periods.

- *Hot flashes and night sweats*: These sudden feelings of intense heat, often accompanied by sweating, can disrupt sleep and daily activities.
- *Mood swings*: Hormonal fluctuations can lead to mood swings, irritability, anxiety, and even depression.
- *Sleep disturbances*: Many women experience difficulties falling asleep or staying asleep during perimenopause.
- *Vaginal changes*: The vaginal walls may become drier, thinner, and less elastic, leading to discomfort during sexual intercourse.
- *Changes in libido*: Some women may experience a decrease in sexual desire during this stage.
- *Urinary problems*: Perimenopause can contribute to urinary tract infections, increased frequency of urination, or urinary incontinence.

***It is important to note that not all women will experience these symptoms, and their severity can vary from person to person.

Dating Meno: The Menopause Stage

As Hope's relationship with Meno (menopause) begins, she realizes that the irregularity of her periods has ceased, and she is now in the menopause stage. The hot flashes and mood swings have become more manageable, and Hope has learned to adapt to her new normal.

In this stage, **Menopause: The Transition's Culmination**

Menopause is officially diagnosed when a woman has gone twelve consecutive months without menstruation. The average age of menopause in the United States is around 51 years old, but it can occur earlier or later depending on several factors, including genetics, overall health and even stress. Symptoms that may accompany menopause include:

- **Absence of periods**: Menstruation ceases completely during menopause.
- **Vasomotor symptoms**: Hot flashes (flushes) and night sweats may continue or worsen during menopause.
- **Sleep disturbances**: Sleep problems, such as insomnia, can persist into menopause.
- **Mood changes**: Hormonal fluctuations can lead to mood swings, irritability, anxiety, and depression.
- **Physical changes**: Some women may experience weight gain, changes in body shape, or thinning hair.
- **Bone density loss**: Estrogen plays a crucial role in maintaining bone health, so its decline during menopause increases the risk of osteoporosis.
- **Sexual changes**: Vaginal dryness and decreased libido may persist or worsen during menopause.

Marrying Post: The Post menopause Stage

Finally, Hope transitions into marriage with Post and enters the post menopause stage. Her symptoms from Perimenopause and Menopause such as hot flashes (flushes) and mood swings have subsided, and she feels more confident and empowered. Hope has learned to embrace the natural changes her body has gone through and is now enjoying the freedom that comes with this new phase in her life.

In this stage, **Post menopause: Life After Menopause**

Post menopause refers to the period following menopause. At this stage, hormone levels have stabilized at their new low levels. While many symptoms experienced during perimenopause and menopause may diminish or disappear altogether, some long-term effects can still be present:

- **Osteoporosis**: The risk of developing osteoporosis remains elevated post menopause due to reduced estrogen levels.
- **Cardiovascular health**: The decline in estrogen also affects cardiovascular health, potentially increasing the risk of heart disease and stroke.
- **Genitourinary changes**: Vaginal dryness, urinary tract infections, and urinary incontinence may persist in postmenopausal women.
- **Emotional well-being**: Some women may experience a sense of loss or a shift in identity as they adapt to life after menopause.
- **Long-term consequences**: Menopause has been associated with an increased risk of certain health conditions, such as cognitive decline, mood disorders, and certain cancers.

In conclusion, the menopause transition can be compared to the love story of Hope, as she experiences distinct stages of her life with *Peri, Meno, and Post*. Each stage is marked by unique experiences and emotions, much like the different phases in a love story. It is important to get a better understanding and appreciation of the journey one takes through the menopause transition. It is equally important to seek support and make plans for the things you love until the end of time.

Start with a vision statement plan for yourself of the things that are most important to you. Write down a vision of how you want to spend the rest of your life. This should include self-care that addresses your physical, mental, emotional, financial, and social needs.

It is important for women going through menopause to be kind to themselves, show self-compassion, and avoid self-sabotage or self-criticism. By taking inspiration from Hope's experience of embracing the transition of menopause and finding happiness, we can learn valuable lessons about navigating this phase of life.

Let us see how her love story ends......

Hope's Life After Marriage: Finding Inner Beauty and Happiness

Hope's journey to self-love and self-worth started when she realized that she needed to take care of herself to be the best version of herself. This realization led her to embark on a journey that would not only improve her physical appearance but also her mental and emotional well-being.

Nutrition

One of the first steps Hope took in this journey was **focusing on proper nutrition.** She began researching healthy eating habits and balanced diets, ensuring that she was consuming all the necessary nutrients to maintain a healthy weight and feel her best. This included **eating slowly and savoring her food**, which allowed her to appreciate the flavors and textures more fully as well as **help mitigate digestive issues and symptoms** because of the tremendous stress caused by her relationships with Peri, Meno and Post. She ate **more protein** and made sure to **have it with every meal**. Her diet was composed of mostly **whole grain food, fermented foods, fruits, and vegetables**. She limited her starchy carbohydrates (pasta, rice, bread, etc.) and sugar, but did have it. She made sure to have a **good probiotic/ prebiotic** daily. Since her reproductive system no longer works, meaning a permanent decline in estrogen and progesterone from her ovaries, she **ate more foods with these properties and herbal teas** to help support and balance her hormones.

Exercise And Movement

Another important aspect of Hope's journey was incorporating **daily physical activities** and exercise into her routine. She discovered that engaging in regular physical activity not only helped her maintain a healthy weight but also improved her mood and overall well-being. Her routine was daily moderate-intensity exercises such as brisk walking, aerobics, biking, and dancing. Twice a week she lifted weights and once a week, she did a short HIIT workout. **She did 20 minutes or LESS of any workout except when she walked, she did 30 minutes.** She learned that less is best as more may cause more stress in her body. Hence, more inflammation or poor recovery results in weight gain. She found what worked best for her by consulting with a fitness coach who specializes in 'women going through the menopause transition.' At the end of the day, by finding activities that she enjoyed, such as hiking, swimming, and yoga, she was able to stay motivated and committed to her fitness goals.

Meditation

Meditation also played a significant role in Hope's journey. By dedicating time each day to practice mindfulness and self-reflection, she was able to reduce stress (cortisol levels), increase her mental clarity, and gain a better understanding of her emotions.

***Cortisol is a type of hormone known as a steroid hormone that is produced by the adrenal glands, which are located on top of the kidneys. Cortisol is commonly referred to as the "stress hormone" because its levels in the body tend to increase in response to stress. It plays a crucial role in various physiological processes and engages in the regulation of metabolism, immune response, inflammation, and stress response.

Through meditation, Hope was able to reduce her "stress hormone" which helped her become more resilient when faced with mental, physical, and emotional challenges.

Quality Time with Others

Quality time with her husband, children, grandchildren, family, and friends was another essential component of Hope's journey. She made a conscious effort to prioritize these relationships and invest time in nurturing them. This not only brought her happiness and contentment but also strengthened her emotional resilience.

Hope also recognized the importance of **taking excursions and vacations** that brought her joy and happiness. By doing so, she was able to break away from her daily routine, recharge her batteries, and appreciate the beauty of the world around her. This helped her maintain a positive outlook on life and feel grateful for the experiences and people she had in her life.

As a result of her journey, Hope never looked better. She maintained a healthy weight, had more energy, and experienced less stress. She was able to face mental, physical, and emotional challenges with greater ease, thanks to her newfound sense of self-worth and the support of her loved ones.

In conclusion, Hope's journey to self-love and self-worth was a transformative experience that allowed her to become the best version of herself. By focusing on proper nutrition, daily physical activities, exercise, meditation, and quality time with loved ones, she was able to find inner beauty and happiness, leading to a more fulfilling and contented life.

WHAT ABOUT YOU?
WHAT WORKS FOR YOU?

Below Are Tips That May Work:

1. **Understand the Menopause Transition** AND Embrace It! Learn to say, "It's not me, it's MENOPAUSE."

2. **Develop a Vision Statement Plan** for yourself what is most important to you. What you want to do and accomplish until the end of life.

3. **Maintain a Healthy Lifestyle** to include nutrition, exercise and GETTING ENOUGH SLEEP (minimum of 7 hours).

    Leading a healthy lifestyle is essential for women going through menopause. Eating a balanced diet, exercising regularly, and getting enough sleep can help alleviate some of the symptoms associated with this transition. Moderate exercise of 15 – 20 minutes 5 days a week. (i.e., dance, aerobics, lightweight training, low-impact workout, no more than 15 minutes HIIT, walking, etc.) can help women maintain a healthy weight. Additionally, eating more whole grain foods, lean protein, and fiber (fruits and vegetables) helps.

Note that it is important to maintain a healthy weight as it can help **reduce the risk of developing chronic conditions, such as heart disease and diabetes.**

Authoritative Reference Title 2: WebMD - Menopause and Lifestyle Changes WebMD offers advice on how to maintain a healthy lifestyle during menopause, including tips on diet, exercise, and sleep. This resource provides women with practical strategies to improve their overall well-being during this time.

4. Stay Hydrated

Staying hydrated is crucial for women going through menopause, as it can help alleviate some of the common symptoms, such as hot flashes (flushes) and night sweats. Drinking plenty of water throughout the day can also help regulate body temperature and maintain overall health.

Authoritative Reference Title 3: Harvard Health - The Importance of Hydration During Menopause This article from Harvard Health explains the importance of staying hydrated during menopause and offers tips on how to increase water intake to stay healthy and comfortable.

5. Manage Stress

Stress can exacerbate menopause symptoms and negatively impact overall well-being. Practicing stress management techniques, such as meditation, deep breathing, and yoga, can help women better cope with the physical and emotional challenges of menopause.

Authoritative Reference Title 4: Cleveland Clinic - Managing Stress During Menopause the Cleveland Clinic provides information on stress management techniques specifically tailored for women going through menopause. This resource offers practical advice on how to reduce stress and improve mental and emotional health during this transitional period.

6. Consider Hormone Replacement Therapy (HRT)

Hormone replacement therapy can help alleviate some menopause symptoms, such as hot flashes (flushes) and night sweats. However, it is essential to discuss the potential risks and benefits of HRT with a healthcare professional before starting treatment.

Authoritative Reference Title 5: National Institute on Aging - Hormone Therapy for Menopause The National Institute on Aging offers a detailed overview of hormone replacement therapy for menopause, including its benefits and risks. This resource helps women make informed decisions about whether HRT is the right choice for them.

7. Explore Alternative Treatments

In addition to HRT, there are alternative treatments available for menopause symptoms. These may include herbal remedies, acupuncture, and bioidentical hormones. Women should consult with a healthcare professional before trying any alternative treatments to ensure they are safe and appropriate for their individual needs.

Authoritative Reference Title 6: American College of Obstetricians and Gynecologists - Alternative Therapies for Menopause, The American College of Obstetricians and Gynecologists provides an overview of alternative treatments for menopause symptoms, including information on their safety, effectiveness, and potential side effects. This resource helps women make informed decisions about which treatments may be best for them.

8. Seek Support and Encouragement

Menopause can be an isolating and challenging experience for many women. It is essential to seek support from friends, family, or a support group to share experiences, advice, and encouragement.

Authoritative Reference Title 7: National Women's Health Information Center - Menopause Support Groups The National Women's Health Information Center offers a list of resources for women seeking support during menopause, including online forums, local support groups, and hotlines. This resource helps women connect with others who understand the unique challenges they face during this transitional period.

About the Author

Eunice Gibson-Hudson is a multi-faceted individual with a diverse background. She is a Christian, a mother of three and mother-figure to her niece, and a wife. She is a graduate of the University of Miami, which indicates her commitment to education and personal development. Her professional experience includes working as a business and non-profit consultant, highlighting her expertise in organizational management and strategic planning. Additionally, she has a background in medical social work, indicating her understanding of the healthcare system and patient care. She is a health and wellness coach certified in senior fitness, demonstrating her dedication to promoting physical well-being among older adults. Furthermore, she is currently pursuing certification in menopause and women's fitness, highlighting her commitment to understanding and addressing the unique health needs of women experiencing menopause.

In her personal life, the author has a passion for softball and competes in women's 50 and over tournaments across the United States. Her active participation in competitive sports reflects her commitment to maintaining an active and healthy lifestyle. Notably, she is the only woman in the women's senior softball division to hold her own signature bat called Daisy, which has earned her the nickname "Daisy" within the softball community. She is married to the softball legendary Robert L. Hudson aka 'Long Ball Billy' who is a two-time hall of famer and too holds a signature bat and another shared with other legends.

The combination of her professional expertise in business consulting, medical social work, and health coaching, along with her firsthand experiences as a mother, wife, and athlete, likely informs her perspective on menopause. Her diverse background suggests that she brings a comprehensive approach to understanding and addressing the physical, emotional, and social aspects of menopause which has influenced her writing of this book.

Made in the USA
Coppell, TX
30 March 2024

30728968R00015